SAFER

Written by
Sarah Jane Dickenson

SAFER
Sarah Jane Dickenson

All rights reserved. No part of this book may be reproduced, stored in a retrieval system or transmitted in any form or by any means electronic, mechanical, photocopying, recording or otherwise, without the prior permission of the publisher.

ISBN 978-1-903110-35-5

First published in this edition 2022 by Wrecking Ball Press.

Copyright Sarah Jane Dickenson

Cover image: Angelo Irving and Ethan Lang in *Safer*.
Photograph by Lucy Fielding.

Sarah Jane Dickenson has asserted her moral rights to be identified as the author of this play in accordance with section 77 of the Copyright, Designs & Patents act 1988.

All rights whatsoever in this play are strictly reserved. Application for professional and amateur performance in any medium and in any language should be made before commencement of rehearsals and, in the first instance, should be addressed to the author at sjdickenson@outlook.com

No performance may be given without a license being granted and no alterations may be made to the title or the text of the play without the author's prior written consent.

For The Roundheads

Safer is based on the true stories of International Gay Rugby Union (IGR) players which were gathered in the spring of 2022. A big thank you goes out to all those who were willing to be interviewed and brave in their candid honesty.

Safer was first toured in 2022 in Hull and at the Commonwealth Games in Birmingham with the following creative team:

Director: Lucy Fielding
Writer: Sarah Jane Dickenson
All characters played by: Angelo Irving & Ethan Lang
Producers: David Eldridge & Matthew Sedman

The creative team of Safer would like to thank the University of Hull and The Ideas Fund. The Ideas Fund is delivered by the British Science Association (BSA) and funded by Wellcome.

CHARACTERS

Michael

Matt

Butterfly Boy

Nick

Banter Boy 1

Banter Boy 2

Reporter

Chair

Rudi

Dan

Straight Player

James

Davy

Nasty Man

Player/Teacher

Two actors can play all characters.

There is no scenery, no mime. The focus is entirely on the drama of the scene.

There is much direct address.

/ means the next line interrupts.

... At the end of speech means it tails off. On its own it indicates a thought moment or pres-sure/uncertain desire to speak.

A line with no full stop at the end of the speech means the next speech follows on immediately.

A character with no dialogue and a - is deliberately remaining silent.

The text has been punctuated to serve the music of the play, not grammatical convention.

Place names can be substituted for others in future productions.

MICHAEL & MATT.

Michael   Michael - Matt -

Matt   Matt - Michael -

Michael   I was having a beer, scrolling.
Facebook - Grindr, etc. Saw the post. I kind of thought A gay' rugby team, is that me? Really? So I had another beer. And then I read it properly and thought 'Oh, actually'…

Matt   It's gay AND inclusive and there's a league out there and it's all this stuff that's, that I thought - well that so absolutely could be me.

Michael   Don't get me wrong I wanted it to work but - I couldn't reply for a bit.

Matt   I remember responding immediately.
'Amazing! - I put -'I'm super interested!'.
And then they set up a meeting.

Michael   I thought, Bet it's just a couple of us in a room saying 'God, it's going to be really hard to recruit' -

Matt   And we got there and we totally filled this huge function room. Everyone was super excited, super enthusiastic. Honestly, it was electric. People pitching in, volunteering even for things they probably didn't know how to do.

Michael   *(aside)* Say that again.

Matt   People were going, 'right, do you want to be a treasurer' - marketing? And you're like, 'Oh my God. That's a really big, important job'.

Michael   Bigger than my ACTUAL job!

Matt   But people were genuinely desperate to get it going, and that thing of, just know-ing, straight away, as soon as we are all together in that room, just knowing that -

Michael   That all of us together - had very, very, VERY little rugby experience.

Matt   What was super amazing -It wasn't that we were rugby players joining something for the rugby. It was LGBTQ+ people and allies that wanted to - to make something happen.

Michael   I thought - Well I guess we can run around a bit – exercise.

Matt   Better than relying on Grindr.

Michael   Er - actually -

Matt   We voted in the Chair.

Michael   Do they have a name?

Matt   They said - right a training session - lets do a training session - everyone saying 'yeh let's do it!'

Michael   I thought, they SAY that but when it comes to training - I mean - this is Hull in winter - that North Sea wind can rip your nipples off let alone your -

Matt   Our first training session was booked for a Friday.

Michael It was pissing it down - I thought 'how many will turn up? 10 - 5 - me and a dog - not even the dog in this rain'.

Matt And there was at least about 30 people, maybe more!

Michael I thought - 'well'.

Matt And I was like, 'Oh my God, like, this is amazing'. Pride always makes me quite emotional, but this. We thought it'd be a struggle, and actually people wanted it, needed it.

Michael You started blubbing.

Matt There was a tear in your eye.

Michael North - bloody -sea wind that.

Matt So the Team was born.

CHANGE. A CAR IN A CAR PARK. **BUTTERFLY BOY.**

Butterfly Boy   I'll give it a try.
I'll give it a try.
I'll give it a try...
It's so far out of my comfort zone. So far.
So far. So far, so fuck-right off far.
-

What am I thinking. Sitting in a Fiat-500 in the pouring - no torrential rain.
Can't see through the bloody windscreen
Turn around.
Just turn around, go home.
This isn't
Just isn't for you
It's going to be
Wet
And cold
And full of people you don't know.
So just turn the car around
Start the bloody thing, turn the wipers on, Put it into gear
And -
Ooh. A person. Are they an inclusive rugby player..?
Idiot!
I mean why would they look like a...
Everybody is a rugby body right.
Should I go and say hi to them?
Oh god that could be so embarrassing on so many...
-

OK, I'm going to step out - step out of the car
Into the absolutely torrential pissing rain
and go in...casually
Step out.

GO IN.
Im going in.
-
-
So I go in.
like, honestly that decision...
if there's any decision I've ever made that led to a butterfly effect...
Getting out of that car changed my life.
So much.
I mean, If I'd have gone home...Honestly!

CHANGE. 1985. **NICK, BANTER BOY 1, BANTER BOY 2.**

Nick 1985 - Secondary school. Boys changing rooms. Rugby practice. I'm Nick age 15. I'm in the corner head down eyes firmly on my blue adidas kit bag. Changing as fast as possible. Chat starts.

Banter Boy 1 Did you get any last night?

Banter Boy 2 Bet *you* didn't.

Banter Boy 1 Bet I did!

Banter Boy 2 I got tit.

Banter Boy 1 I got tit last week! But this week - smell that.

He shoves his fingers under **Banter Boy 2**'s *nose.*

Banter Boy 2 Eeeewww! That stinks!

Banter Boy 1 Fanny that. Haven't washed my hands.

Banter Boy 2 Who was it?

Banter Boy 1 *(making it up)* Tracey Turner.

Banter Boy 2 Thought I recognised the smell. That scrubber don't wash. You might catch something!

Nick Loud laughter - pushing - shoving - someone fell against me - you have to react - Oi! Watch it!

Banter Boy 1 Watch it yourself bum boy!

Nick Always react- if you don't react - you're the Bender - shirt lifter! *(Loud laughter)* - then keep changing - eyes back on bag - feeling, feeling...

CHANGE. **REPORTER** *&* **CHAIR.**

Reporter   Hi guys, thanks for turning up at stupid o'clock to record this, and so many of you. Really appreciate it. I just need to set up my kit - cut backs eh I'm on my lonesome - But I'll chat on - bit of background - viewers want background - and you are...?

Chair   I'm the Chair, Thank you so much for this it's great for the club to be seen on TV.

Reporter   Right in thinking it's Union?

Chair   Yes.

Reporter   Rugby Union.

Chair   Yes.

Reporter   In a League obsessed city?

Chair   Yes.

Reporter   Okey dokey - So - Chair. What are you?

Chair   Sorry?

Reporter   I have to get my head around the questions - sometimes daft and definitely blunt - that my viewers - not me - will be asking - demanding - answers to. So are you gay, straight, trans, what?

Chair   I self identify as gay.

Reporter   So why an 'inclusive' team - that's the word isn't it 'inclusive'.

Chair   Well it means that everyone feels they are welcomed to play rugby however you self identify -

Reporter   'Self...identify', 'Self-identify' just trying to get my mouth around it - for the viewers - don't judge me - But we've got loads of mens teams, women's teams some good some not so- surely there's a team for everyone already, I mean some are really rubbish.

Chair   We're competitive, just not intimidating -

Reporter   So inclusive can mean soft - well it is union - just asking what my viewers will be asking - probably shouting - at the screen.

Chair   But sometimes, the atmosphere can be a bit toxic.

Reporter   It's rugby - got to assert yourself - intimidate.

Chair   But not your team mates, we hope -

Reporter   Great Chair thanks that gives me an in -
Can I talk to a straight one now or is there a trans one about - not fussed which.

CHANGE. 1996. DAN, BANTER BOY 1, BANTER BOY 2.

Dan   1996 Secondary school. Boys changing rooms. Rugby practice. I'm Dan aged 17. I'm in the corner head down eyes firmly on the red Nike kit bag. Chat starts.

Banter boy 1   Did you get any last night?

Banter boy 2   What E or a shag?

Banter boy 1   I had both.

Banter boy 2   I'm still buzzing.

Banter boy 1   Can't have had a proper shag then.

Banter boy 2   All about the dancing me. But a slapper sucked me off outside the bogs -

Banter boy 1   Who?

Banter boy 2   *(making it up)* Jessica Jones - then I'm straight back on the floor giving it large *(dance moves)*.

Banter boy 1   Sure it wasn't some queer in the bogs?

Dan   Loud laughter - pushing - shoving - someone fell against me - you have to react - Oi watch it!

Banter boy 2   Sorreeee. Didn't see you there tosspot, oh right you never go out. Wanking to the Spice Girls on MTV *(singing/gesturing - 'I wanna (ha) I wanna (ha) I wanna (ha) I wanna (ha) I wanna really, really, really zigazigzag'ah!)*. Or was it Take That?!

Dan Truthfully - it was George Michael - but always react - if you don't react - 'talking about yourself gay boy got pictures of Backstreet Boys - faggot features!'
Loud laughter - keep changing - eyes on the bag - feeling...

Banter boy 2 Eh - just messing - bit heavy mate - cant' you take a joke.

CHANGE. **REPORTER & STRAIGHT PLAYER.**

Reporter   I can see by the tools hanging down from your belt you're a working man.

Straight Player   Er, yes.

Reporter   So - let me get this right - you are straight?

Straight Player   Yes.

Reporter   So. Why a 'gay' rugby team?

Straight Player   It's an inclusive rugby team.

Reporter   Hold on, other players have said 'gay' /

Straight Player   / Inclusive.

Reporter   Gay inclusive.

Straight Player   Yeh. Inclusive.

Reporter   'Inclusive' - not exactly a catchy title

Straight Player   Does it have to be?

Reporter   'Gay', people remember, 'inclusive' - meh. My viewers will ask - definitely ask - Could you not get into straight teams?

Straight Player   I did.

Reporter   Not good enough?

Straight Player   My mate came here and he said they were friendly so..

Reporter   Your friend is what? Gay, straight, trans -

Straight Player   A plumber.

Reporter   - So how do you find playing with an 'inclusive' team

Straight Player   Kinda weird -

Reporter   Weird ok - Yes! I see my viewers nodding - really nodding - so 'weird' how? -

Straight Player   Dunno just -

Reporter   Got to put your side, loud and clear.

Straight Player   Me, playing for other teams - I had to be ...

Reporter   Aggressive?

Straight Player   No -

Reporter   Fierce?

Straight Player   No -

Reporter   A leader?

Straight Player   A bit of an arse.

Reporter Right.

Straight Player As a straight man, joining this team - inclusive team - you have to learn.
You have to learn - where boundaries are. 'Cos you come in as - well straight.
So you probably need to be a bit...

Reporter Wary?

Straight Player No.

Reporter Watchful?

Straight Player No.

Reporter Scared?

Straight Player Humble. Be a bit humble when you come in.

Reporter Humble! C'mon, rugby is so not about being humble right. I mean, I know, I used to play.

Straight Player What position?

Reporter Captain. You need your leaders right, who know how to -

Straight Player Intimidate.

Reporter Yeh. Yeh, intimidate.
Intimidate the other team, intimidate the Ref,

intimidate anyone slacking.

Straight Player Own teammates?

Reporter Look, I'm not apologising, I played hard.

Straight Player Intimidated hard.

Reporter Yeh.

Straight Player Bit of an arse then.

CHANGE. 2017. JAMES, BANTER BOY 1 & BANTER BOY 2.

James   2017 - University. Men's changing rooms. First rugby practice. James aged 18. I'm in the corner head down eyes firmly on my new under-armour kit bag. Changing as fast as possible. Must be different here - surely - I mean - we are the future, future plan-ners, teachers, lawyers, politicians future leaders of everything...Banter starts.

Banter Boy 1   Alright ladies! Initiation night tonight!

Banter Boy 2   All plans are in place and even though I am the fecking Social Secs for the team they are friggin' amazing!

Banter Boy 1   Man, I was completely wankered after last year.

Banter Boy 2   Yeh, he's not joking!

   Laughter.

Banter Boy 1   So not, my arse was sore for days.

Banter Boy 2   Sure that wasn't your boyfriend!

Banter Boy 1   You are so gay! So looking forward to getting my own back this year with you new ladies.

Banter Boy 2   And if things turn out as planned we can finish off with the girls hockey team.

Banter Boy 1   Didn't one of you piss on some of them last year - bit of a blur.

Banter Boy 2 It was only a forfeit.

Banter Boy 1 Or 'cos we can.

Banter Boy 2 But hey, that's team bonding for you.

Banter Boy 1 And they were really pissed so... But rule is - Only rule is -

Banter Boy 2 What happens during initiation stays -

Banter Boy 1 On WhatsApp! Those girls have so not lived it down!

Banter Boy 2 You are seriously gay!

Banter Boy 1 Look at your faces - just banter ladeez just / bantaaah!

Banter Boy 2 / Bantaaah!

James I kept changing - eyes back on bag - I didn't react - said nothing - nothing - feeling....feeling just...

CHANGE. **REPORTER & DAVY.**

Reporter So let me get this right, you are -

Davy Davy.

Reporter Davy, right, so you are a -

Davy A prop.

Reporter Right a prop. We need our props.

Davy Never thought I'd be a prop - ever.

Reporter Good but you are a -

Davy My mum said I could be anything I ever wanted. Mum's eh.

Reporter Mums eh. So, you're -

Davy Super supportive my Mum.

Reporter Great. So you're a - what a -

Davy Social Secretary. Organise everything off the field. Mind you this group are super sociable -always coming up with ideas - dead easy.

Reporter Yes but you're also -

Davy Oh yeh! I'm committee Convener.

Reporter Right.

Davy Sounds posh I know but it's super straight forward.

Reporter Right but my viewers -

Davy Yeh, course. Not all of them will be across this.

Reporter Exactly. Need the basics, so you are -

Davy Talkative. So Committee Convener, It helps if your talkative - get everyone talking - I'm super talkative.

Reporter Really.

Davy If someone is unhappy, I immediately call a committee meeting or a team meeting where things are discussed. Little things, big things - works for us. I know other teams - more established teams are not so gentle but inclusive - takes all sorts.

Reporter EXACTLY. So what are you? Gay, straight -

Davy I'm a Trans man.

Reporter Right so -

Davy What are you?

Reporter Oh, didn't I? Duh - sorry - I'm a reporter - TV reporter.

Davy I know. But - What are you?

CHANGE. **BUTTERFLY BOY.**

Butterfly Boy   Before I got out of that Fiat 500 - in the rain.
I was the epitome of a gay man - in air quotes "not like other gay men".
I guess I would portray myself a lot more...
My interests,
my mannerisms were a lot more,
I guess, *(in air quotes)* "masculine".
I prided myself on that.

I didn't watch Drag Race, or go to gay clubs. I did, *(in air quotes,)* "the norm".
So I adapted myself to a norm that wasn't, I guess, me.
And then well -
I got out the car.
I mean,
that big beautiful fuck-right-off butterfly -
I mean, I got my first "real" relationship.
And bugger me he watched Drag Race! and I would be like,
"How could you watch this?"
I mean - shameful of me or what.
-
And next thing you know, like,
I'm watching Drag Race
AND I'm doing drag!
I've been out in drag and absolutely love it!
Not all the time obvs,
The heels kill me and are not great on the hammies if you want to keep match fit.
But you know, it's something that I would have never, ever, EVER, had done.
First episode of Drag Race - tick
First time in drag - tick
Oh yeh and

First queer film seen - tick
First queer book read - tick
And, you know, before,
I wouldn't have read one of those watched one of those
And now, I'm absolutely obsessed! But you know what?
Every time I do something like that, I have this moment like...
If I hadn't got out of my car that day, I would not
Absolutely not
Be here strutting
my rugby fit bear body, wearing fuck-right-off amazing dangly earrings on the streets of Hull.

And you know what?
I feel
A "better person".
Yeah, totally.
One hundred percent.

CHANGE. 2018. JAMES & CHAIR.

James   2018. Some drafty port-a-cabin. Changing rooms. Rugby practice. Still James now aged 19. I'm in the corner head down eyes firmly on my Lidl bag as my Under-Armor kit bag - couldn't get the smell of piss out. Changing as fast as possible.

Chair   Hi.

James   Hi.

Chair   Good you could come.
I'm 'The Chair'. I do have a name, but no one uses it.
Not even my mum!

James   Right

Chair   Don't often call me Chair either - teasing y'know -

James   Right but -

Chair   'Hey Lazy Boy!' That's one -

James   Yes but -

Chair   'Hey rocking!' You know rocking chair - I use Skunk Anansie for warm up -

James   But -

Chair   They prefer Britney -

James   The team!

Chair   Yes - sorry -

James   Inclusive right?

Chair   Inclusive - definitely. I'm gay but we have straight, bi, trans gender, pansexual, whatever, oh and we have Rudi - you'll notice the accent - who is the grandad of the team but probably the fittest, have you played before?

James   Sort of.

Chair   Some have a little, some have a lot and some - well - like me. I did Art. Position?

James   Sorry?

Chair   That you play?

James   Second row.

Chair   Cool.

James   Is there -

Chair   Space, course, we rotate - share positions anyway.

James   No, is there…

Chair   Is there…?

James   Initiation stuff.

Chair Well...

James Right.

Chair Some of us go for a drink afterwards, some do some don't, People are pretty laid back about it. But sometimes - and I feel I must warn you -

James Oh. Right.

Chair Quiz night.

James Quiz night?

Chair Things can get a bit - the teachers - librarians - hate losing.

James Right.

Chair They usually lose. Know nothing about gaming -
Are you from here?

James No. But...

Chair But?

James I - *(plucking up courage)*
I'm gay and - James - and gay - at Uni here.

Chair Jolly good.
Uni student - we have a few of them also police, electrician, builders, people in between jobs and some... haven't a clue, *(looking at watch)*

but Coach'll be in soon, we best get a wiggle on - get changed.

James So. Eyes back firmly on my Lidl bag for life, Changing as fast as possible, but this time, this time...feeling...
I wanted to, I really, really, really wanted to.

CHANGE. DAVY.

Davy Hi - Davy again. Alright? My Mum -
Super friendly my Mum. Always got talking to people
From the off She was like, looking for teams, clubs for me - I mean I didn't know what I was - but Mum figured it was the gender stuff I needed help with.
Super smart my mum.

Because where I grew up, there was no - Oh I knew gay people existed and I knew trans people existed - but I just thought it was really, really rare.
And I just thought, 'Well, I might meet, like, one, in my life.'

I was that kid did every after school sports club, every team. Loved it!
And Mum came and watched - Like everything.
She worked full time an' all
Don't know how she did it
Most parents were drop and go.

I tried playing rugby
Bit problematic because I was like, pre all my transition stuff. So I was...
I had my old name, and, but I was like, big, stocky not-a-girl but a girl, short hair, wore guys clothes.
Mum said, 'Tell 'em'.'
So I did. I'd see 'em looking and I'd say -
'I want to be a boy'.
Which worked - for a bit

Once, some parent said - I mean mum and me standing there
'Well of course you're going to win, you've got a boy on your team.'
Actually I quite liked that - me taken for a boy - but mum was super sharp.
'That's great you think that, 'cos they've had no help yet.'
And gave her that 'mum stare.' *(shows)*

But - in my heart...
I so didn't want to be playing in the girls team, I was desperate to play in the boy's team.
So I just...
I couldn't do teams anymore.

So. Mum took me to Pride in town.
And I was like Wow!
And I met my first trans person
I mean whaaaat!
That was massive!
Because I'd just
I'd gone to get ice creams - it was that hot
And there I was with melting 99's looking for Mum and there she was chatting to them like she'd known them all their life
And they loved her.
Wished their Mum was like her.
And then the Chair came along
Mum thought him super nice too.
There's a team you can join' mum said.
'You'll be safer' she said. She so wanted me to be super safe...
-
My sister is super amazing.
Brings my nephews to see my matches - to show them.
And they see their mum cheering me on - super, super loud!
They see her taking the piss a bit too -
But hey - she's my sister.
Families eh.
Mum...
She would have loved it.

CHANGE. **MICHAEL.**

Michael Michael again - see - no Matt.
He still goes but me...
I mean I gave it a go. But I found it a bit...
There's this group there - in the team. Always put their hands up for anything - real quick. I mean...I want to but... told Matt I need to think a bit before I...you know.
Same ones
Always the same ones
Hands shoot up.
If I'm honest...
Bit of a clique.
Yeh, that's it, a clique.
Not good at cliques me.
Matt says their not a clique just enthusiastic.
Says they get things done,
not cynical...
So, there was me, changing, getting on with it,
and them, all changing, giggling, messing.
Matt messing with them...
Like I said he still goes - loves it - keeps him really busy.
But me...I jog.

CHANGE. **RUDI & NASTY MAN.**

Rudi   Hi - I'm Rudi. Age - depends on the day. The accent. You noticed?
Been here a while though.

   Enter **Nasty Man.**

Nasty Man   My name? None of your business.
I didn't linger.
Didn't want to.
Just one training session.
Only one reason I went.

Rudi   Yes I know, I can come across as fairly camp. When I was a teen, everybody thought I was gay and I kind of accepted that.
I even thought, 'oh, I'm probably gay'. So, I tried for a long time being gay. And then it turned out it wasn't actually for me, but I had already been part of all these networks and communities and people. And it never really stopped in my life. And so I make a point of saying I'm straight, but I'm kind of Queer-socialized.

I LOVE physical contact!
Being with this team gives me TWO types of physical contact:

ONE, is a lot of hugging, it's a very huggy team. Very physically affectionate... In a non-creepy way. Just hugs and kisses for greetings. Very European, very positive thing.

Nasty Man   At College he did all that chat stuff girls love, you know, Chat, chat, chat, chat, about complete bollocks - and they'd laugh and flirt with him even though - and ignore you an'-
So fucking annoying -

With his flicky wavy black hair and different clothes and smart mouth.
He had such a smart mouth.
Had a comeback whatever you said whatever you did and - I mean - I said - and did a lot.

Rudi TWO, tackling.
I love tackling - I love being tackled.
I like the risks involved with that. I like the pain. It's...
Am I sounding a bit weird?
You look like you're thinking
'He is sounding a bit weird'.
Listen.
If, you in your working life have to be reasonable and understanding all the time and I do
I mean, ALL THE TIME,
Then it's actually great fun to have an excuse to NOT be that reasonable and understanding and treat people in a way you wouldn't treat them in your working life.

Nasty Man What really pissed me off was he was good at sports. Any sport.
No - no - what TOTALLY pissed me off was he wasn't BOTHERED - about sport.
'I don't have the competitive gene' he'd say.
I did.
Tried to show him competitive. But he'd dance out of any tackle taking the piss with that smart mouth.

Rudi You make a contract in rugby that there is risk and you're going to get physical.
You make a contract saying: 'It's OK, I may hurt you, but you may hurt

me and we want to do that now'. The contract keeps you safe - keeps us safe - apart from a few broken bones.

But if you get someone who doesn't stick to the contract...

Nasty Man   Still competitive me. I'm down that gym every single day - even Christmas day - making sure I'm ready - like match ready, no one, I mean no one beats my deadlift. I tell you what - they don't even try now - they back off when I walk towards the equipment... that is how good - how competitive I am.

Rudi   Someone turned up to a training session who seemed to deliberately try to hurt people in tackles.
The question was: was this person deliberately trying to hurt gay men and others they saw as different?
Or was it just someone who wanted to show physical dominance over other people?
Or was he just a bad, bad, character.

Nasty Man   Social media - got hold of him.
He, remembered me.
I gave it the -'hey weren't we all dickheads back then' an''hey great he was playing rugby' and great, great, great bollocks and then I said - get this -
I wanted to be an 'ally'.
And he fell for it - Result!
So I went along to a practice.
And there's me and all these, 'inclusive' players and they begin to chuck it around and he's laughing and joking - still not learnt to keep his smart mouth shut - but they're finding him fucking hilarious -
So I chucked a couple of soft passes like the rest of them and then he

got chucked the ball.
BAM! Totally flattened him!

Rudi The chair asked me to assess the situation

Nasty Man I gave the tosser an 'inclusive'
apology *(finds himself funny)* And
Bam! Flattened another.
Bam! Bam! DOUBLE FUCKING BAM!
I was having a GREAT time!

Rudi He was a bad, bad, BAD character for sure.

Nasty Man I saw a couple of them looking at me whispering but I thought GET THIS - This is proper straight
competitive rugby, watch and learn!

Rudi Like I said it is about a contract.
And he, oh he definitely broke the contract.
So...

> **Rudi** *tackles* **Nasty Man** *- mid tackle -*

Nasty Man Look right...I hadn't played for a bit right, was in between teams - sort of - had injuries - sort of.

> **Rudi** *finishes tackling* **Nasty Man** *who is left gasping for air and dazed on the ground. He pulls himself together - sort of.*

He had an accent
Didn't know 'inclusive' meant foreign as well.

Nasty Man *getting up.*

I'd read that when a shark attacks you, you don't see 'em - just feel like you've been hit by a speeding train.
That foreign bastard was a fucking shark. An' - get this - he said 'Great to have PERMISSION to flatten you, let's go again!'
I couldn't be sure considering my vision was blurred but I think that foreign fuck - as he jogged back - winked at the others.

Rudi Michelle Obama said 'If they go low, we go high'. I love Michelle - love her - so I'm so very ashamed to say...
I went low *(he smiles).*

Nasty Man Anyway. Think I made my point.
So... no need to go back.

CHANGE. STRAIGHT PLAYER & REPORTER.

Straight Player   You're back.

Reporter   I'm Looking for the Chair.

Straight Player   To apologise?

Reporter   Look -

Straight Player   I'm looking.

Reporter   You came across really well.

Straight Player   You think.

Reporter   You had an amazing reaction.

Straight Player   Was a reaction alright.

Reporter   Look -

Straight Player   Still looking.

Reporter   Admittedly not all the viewers are broadminded - but any reaction is better than no reaction

Straight Player   The emails -
Just show the rubbish ones did ya?
Like 'ooooh, I know what goes on in the showers...'
I mean people literally just have showers!

Reporter   You should have seen the others -

Straight Player   There were worse!

Reporter   News is about opinions, argument, debate -

Straight Player   Slagging people off.

Reporter   Look -

Straight Player   Still looking.

Reporter   We need to show a broad range of opinions, you go on about being 'inclusive' we need to be inclusive of all -

Straight Player   Poison.

Reporter   Look - The editing.

Straight Player   What about it.

Reporter   That wasn't me I interview - my boss edits.

Straight Player   -

Reporter   Look, I covered your team -
Who else did that round here - nobody
not the local press, not the radio - nobody -
even my boss didn't want me to.
Look, I raised your profile, fought to get you a 5 minute slot on TV - lunchtime admittedly - but they're just emails, virtual chip paper eh -

Straight Player   And ones on the teams website - social media?

Reporter Block - block!
Look, People get bored, move on.

Straight Player -

Reporter The Chair. I wanted to ask.

Straight Player What.

Reporter If... If I could join.

Straight Player The team?

Reporter Uhuh.

Straight Player You're joking.

Reporter Can't tell jokes. Why I work in news.

Straight Player Why?

Reporter I used to play.

Straight Player Can't get into the straight teams?

Reporter No. Yes. No - look I - I want to be -

Straight Player Chair's busy.

Reporter Right. Okay I'll -

Straight Player   Talking to Sky.

Reporter   Sky?

Straight Player   Sky Sports.
They're covering us -
You AND your emails.

Reporter   They're not my -

Straight Player   Twenty minute slot - prime time. Never know, you might be lucky - might be tomorrow's chip paper.

CHANGE. **PLAYER/TEACHER & BUTTERFLY BOY.**

Player/Teacher (*He is in rugby kit holding a Pride flag*) He's late. He's always late. I love him - almost too much - but he's late.

Butterfly Boy (*He has team shirt on see-through shorts and a harness.. He bounds in full of enthusiasm*)
You got the flag - great! Give it here

    He goes to take the flag.

Player/Teacher What are you wearing?

Butterfly Boy My kit - obvs!

Player/Teacher And.

Butterfly Boy My new harness - d'y'like?

Player/Teacher No!

Butterfly Boy You prefer the old one? You did like the old one.

Player/Teacher No -

Butterfly Boy You so did! I was wearing it at Big Scrum. Remember?

Player/Teacher I know but -

Butterfly Boy You REALLY liked it then.

Player/Teacher I know but -

Butterfly Boy In that room on the balcony.

Player/Teacher I / know -

Butterfly Boy / And the other rooms -

Player/Teacher I know / but

Butterfly Boy I / love those rooms!

Player/Teacher I -

Butterfly Boy I so love the smell of cock!

Player/Teacher That was a kink night!

Butterfly Boy I know there were bears, cubs, otters and (looking) puppies.

Player/Teacher This is Pride!

Butterfly Boy So?

Player/Teacher Where are your shorts?

Butterfly Boy On my bum?

Player/Teacher They're not your team rugby shorts

Butterfly Boy I swear I have not eaten for a week to get into these see-through bad boys

Player/Teacher We are leading the parade!

Butterfly Boy I know! *(takes flag plays provocatively).*

Player/Teacher *(trying to grab flag back)* No! No, no, no, no ,no! Tom's a Policeman, Eli is a nurse, Dave is - well I don't know what he is but he's always busy -

Butterfly Boy They're all out

Player/Teacher Ivan's Russian

Butterfly Boy So?

Player/Teacher You tried to be gay in Russia?

Butterfly Boy But he's here. Escaped

Player/Teacher With his family.

Butterfly Boy He has a rainbow flag in his window

Player/Teacher They think that's to do with the NHS - they all work in it - at the moment

Butterfly Boy He doesn't have to do Pride.

Player/Teacher He won't if he see's you dressed like that.

Butterfly Boy His choice.

Player/Teacher   Is it? And what about Raheem?

Butterfly Boy   I want people to know the real me.

Player/Teacher   You sound like a failed 'celeb' on a reality show.

Butterfly Boy   You sound like the teacher you are.

Player/Teacher   My Art Teacher - made me feel - being me could be ok - Clause 28 was kicking off - he was seen at a protest -

Butterfly Boy   'Cos he did that we can do this.

Player/Teacher   He was made to leave.

Butterfly Boy   That was then.

Player/Teacher   Attacks on gays, trans, they're all up -

Butterfly Boy   Sorry don't doom-scroll the Guardian.

Player/Teacher   Sorry Guardian doesn't do Tik-Tok.

Butterfly Boy   My nephew - at your school - says everyone claims to be bi or gay or or non-binary, trans - even if they're not.

Player/Teacher   Not all schools. And when they leave?
Post-gay it is not.
Heartstoppers it is not.

Butterfly Boy   I watched It's a Sin!

Player/Teacher   The team -
What about the straight players?

Butterfly Boy   What about them?

Player/Teacher   You wear that - people will think they're into that.

Butterfly Boy   They might be?

Player/Teacher   That's / not the -

Butterfly Boy   / They're either allies or they're not.

Player/Teacher   That's so / harsh -

Butterfly Boy   / Pride is about protest - wearing kink if we want to - drag if we want to - wiggling my see through shorts in their feck-off faces if I want to - protest!

Player/Teacher   -

Butterfly Boy   -

Player/Teacher   -

Butterfly Boy   Last night...

Player/Teacher   -

Butterfly Boy   Last night.

Player/Teacher   What about last night?

Butterfly Boy   We went out - as a team - gay, trans, whatever and we - we the team - were gobby and fun - got pissed - our dancing was epic - Theo and Jude had a massive re-lationship drama - as always - and you and me, we had the best sex ever!

Player/Teacher   When we got home.

Butterfly Boy   We were ALL just...us. I want us to BE us.

Player/Teacher   We will be carrying this flag through town in front of a lot of people
wearing our team strip -
This is us.
But it is more than us.
Look, we are trying to do something -
be something - that could be -just maybe - truly new.
There isn't a template for this.

Butterfly Boy   -

Player/Teacher   -

Butterfly Boy   *(producing a puppy mask)* I guess you won't want this then.

CHANGE. **RUDI** & **REPORTER.**

Reporter Some drafty port-a-cabin somewhere. Changing rooms. Rugby practice. Reporter - Alex - sitting - eyes firmly on his old Cotton Oxford and Patrick boots. They don't fit.

Rudi Hi I'm Rudi.

Reporter Hi I'm -

Rudi The Reporter. I know.

Reporter I'm not here as a reporter.

Rudi Good because if you were I would have to kill you.

Reporter -

Rudi *(laughing)* Just joking, we do a lot of joking. I understand you wish to play?

Reporter Yes if that's -

Rudi Absolutely.

Reporter Actually about the -

Rudi You have kit?

Reporter Yes - No - I - bit rubbish eh?

Rudi We have spare - you stand there I'll find you something.

>**Rudi** *starts going through spare kit handing some to* **Reporter** *to try for size in next section.*

Reporter Can I ask - I mean -
I was going to ask the - the - electrician -

Rudi I can do many things, but electrics I cannot.

Reporter No. I was going to ask -

Rudi Ask for his card - he's very good, wired my extension - but talk after the rugby.

Reporter But -

Rudi Have you heard about the contract?

Reporter Contract?

Rudi A flexible contract admittedly but part of the contract is we talk work after the rug-by.

Reporter No problem but -

Rudi No, no, no 'buts' after the -

Reporter Banter!

Rudi Pardon me?

Reporter I was going to ask him - the electrician - about the banter.

Rudi -

Reporter Jokes - teasing - having a -

Rudi I may be foreign but I know what banter is.

Reporter It's just...I don't want to get it wrong.

Rudi I've had many, many, MANY conversations with people about this. Correct me if I'm wrong - I rarely am - I think your question is: what's the difference between straight banter and gay slash inclusive banter.

Reporter Yes!

Rudi Even if the material is the same?

Reporter Is it?

Rudi Anal sex. Jokes about anal sex. Who cracks the joke and how?

Reporter Er yes?

Rudi To be clear banter is part of the contract.

Reporter Is it? Oh, right. So try it out - suck it and see?

Rudi BUT - and this is a key BUT -
I still hold back on most of the banter, because I'm not in the position to really judge what's appropriate and what's not.
If you enter into this world, you have to learn where the boundaries

are, because you come in as a figure of the mainstream, the oppressive culture.

Reporter   I don't want / to be -

Rudi   / The women players when, I talk about this they roll their eyes - say I'm mans-plaining - which is probably true as they have to navigate banter ALL the time
But male players need a bit of mansplaining.
Many expect to be considered...well funny
Although trust me many, many, many men are really not funny -
So I'm mansplaining to you - a straight man -

Reporter   But I -

Rudi   Banter wise - You probably need to be a bit...humble - can you do humble?

Reporter   No I'm -

Rudi   I know, I know it seems at odds with being a rugby player, a rugby player needs to be proud and strong.

Reporter   I'm not sure I'm proud or strong -

Rudi   Proud, strong AND humble.
All part of the / contract.

Reporter   / No!

Rudi   No?

Reporter Yes - not no -
I mean
I'm not sure
I mean I am sure
but
I'm not sure
no
I mean -

Rudi Is this your attempt at banter?

Reporter No.
I'm... *(deep breath)*
I don't think I'm straight.

Rudi -

Reporter -

> **Rudi** *gives* **Reporter** *a team shirt.*

Rudi Get changed. We'll go chuck a ball around, hurt each other a bit, eh?

> *Exit* **Rudi.**

> **Reporter** *starts to get changed.*

Reporter So. I get changed as fast as possible, feeling ...feeling that maybe - this time - I'll be...a better person *(he smiles).*